A Poetry Collection

LOUD THOUGHTS

Cachline Etienne

To awkward black girls who stutter. You deserve to be heard. You are loved. I am you.

Table of Contents

I.

<u>Cut My Hair</u>

So, I cut my hair

Yup,

Chop it off with a care.

You see this hair of mine was a crown; my

crown.

But truly, it only served to weight me down.

Every morning, every night,

That feeling that I had to make it right,

4c hair is 'work'

Raw material that you must go at 'til its

'presentable'

'til its polished, professional,

'til its no longer unconformable.

Cause Lord forbid if you don't do your edges…

But right now,

I'm over it,

Just another burden I don't care to deal with.

So,

I cut my hair, and I didn't care.

Cause you see, my hair isn't a crown

My crown is within

And it shines bright when I walk around.

<u>These tears</u>

See these tears,

They represent your fears.

They make you weak,

Meek,

A little too easy to defeat.

What are you crying for?

People out here going through more.

Black women can't afford to be timorous,

'Specially not when the worlds against us.

That feeling of yours,

You need to throw it out the door.

'Cause, if you're going to make it,

That crying you doing need to quit.

-Love,

Society

<u>Black Women Tears</u>

Her face grows warm,

She'd check twice no one's home.

There she lays in her room alone,

Drowning in sorrow, basking in gloom.

Don't cry baby, you'll be alright.

She tries to stop it,

Leave me alone, she groans.

Doing this feels wrong.

Don't cry baby, you'll let them win the fight.

Her face is on fire, it won't be long now.

And just as expected, the dam breaks.

A single drop rolls down her face,

Her breathing starts to pick up pace.

Don't cry baby, you'll be alright.

You're weak the voices say.

Dang, you're crying over a bad day?

Chile, people done been through so much more.

Girl you stupid. What you crying for?

Don't cry baby, you'll let them win the fight.

The tears are streaming down her face,

She's ok, this is her safe space.

There she can be black, woman, and cry.

And so, she cries.

And cry and cry and cry.

Then she steps outside not wiping her tears and fears away,

Because Black Women Tears are okay

And at this point, she doesn't care what people say.

<u>Black Women Blues</u>

'Black Woman is power…'

'Black Woman is strong…'

'Black Woman don't cower…'

'Black Woman fights wrong…'

Everyone knows that song,

They sing it well

Really, it's an "amazing story" to tell.

But…

Who fights for black women when they're bruised?

When they're beaten down and abused?

What happens when –

'Black Woman is weak…'

'Black Woman is tired…'

'Black Woman too quiet…'

'Black Woman do cower…'

Who protects her?

Is a black woman's worth determined by the amount of trauma she overcomes?

Is she deemed worthy only when she becomes a shield?

Does she ever get a chance to truly heal?

Who cries when the black woman dies? (And does she ever make it to Paradise)

This Is For Girls Like Ruby

This poem is dedicated to girls like Ruby.

Girls whose dark skin turn blue under

moonlight;

Girls burdened with the curse of making things

right;

Girls whose eyes sparkle like the stars in a starry

night;

Girls who never back down without a fight.

This poem is for girls like Ruby,

Always giving,

Always caring,

Always helping,

Always sharing!

This poem is for girls like Ruby,

Who are fed up,

Sick,

Tired,

Of being taken for granted.

Tired,

Of being a shield.

This is for girls like Ruby

That navigates through a world that hates them

with grace,

That refuses to let the world dictate their fate.

This is for girls like Ruby,

Whose self care equals to death,

Whose self interest is automatically selfishness.

I love you.

I care about you.

You are enough.

You deserve to follow your dreams.

This is for girls like Ruby (Baptiste).

<u>GOAT</u>

Simone Biles doesn't need your permission to say
I need a break.

she isn't here for your amusement,

Now, let that bake.

Isn't it strange to want to claim possession of a
body that isn't yours? How you yearn to dictate
and control with force.

I mean,

A striking phenomenon with 37 gold medals to
her name,

Somehow, is being questioned by thousands
who've never won a game.

This internet have y'all bold, challenging, and
insulting women you can't control.

But understand,

Understand,

Simone Biles doesn't need your permission and
never will.

No matter what venom you spew,

what examples you use,

Simone Biles,

Olympic champion,

Owes you nothing!

<u>Skin of Mine</u>

This skin of mine,

This black skin,

Is not a weapon.

But yet you're threatened.

This skin of mine,

This black skin,

Should not be a burden.

But yet my back is loaded, overflowing.

This skin of mine,

This black skin,

Evokes emotion,

Creates commotion,

Even when I do nothing.

This skin of mine,

This black skin,

Is something that I'm born in,

Is something that teaches me lessons that I may

not want to learn,

Is something that shows me realities I may not

want to see,

Is something that teaches me how to be me.

This skin of mine,

This black skin,

Is my reality,

My teacher,

And to many, my sin.

<u>LOUD THOUGHTS</u>

Loud,

Just loud,

My thoughts are too damn loud.

Pounding, screeching, makin a mess,

Wailing, failing, begging me to confess.

but I digress,

its far too much stress.

They resonate loud and clear in my head

but when I try to utter them, they leave me for

dead.

they Jump ships and hide in a hurry,

making things all too blurry.

So, I stand there begging my thoughts to

translate

for once please don't leave me at the stake

but by then its too late

I'm a stammering mess downing in self hate.

And then, when I'm all drained out,

and miserable without a doubt,

they slowly creep out and they begin to shout.

Loudly

Far too loud,

My thoughts are too damn loud.

No Struggle Love

I'm sorry,

But I don't want none of that struggle love.

Cause I done struggle enough,

Cause I'm kind of tired of being tough.

I don't want any lies,

No poverty,

I've had enough of toxicity.

I want communication,

I want growth,

I want planning,

I want hope.

I want happiness not attached and tainted by

pain.

I don't want to be playing the blame game.

I want love,

Just Love,

No Struggle,

Love.

I'm Fine…I promise

What do you call it?

When you're,

Too tired to think,

Too bitter to breathe,

Too angry to see,

Too self-loading to be.

When,

Your misery is a never-ending sea,

When,

You've given up hope for finding peace.

When…

<u>Not Okay</u>

Perhaps the load I'd carried was too much to bear,

Maybe I knew I was spiraling; I just didn't care.

Whatever the reason, whatever the cause

I cannot carry on as normal, at least not without a cost.

I've allowed myself to be anything, once it's for somebody else,

But truly I've only been neglecting myself.

Now I'm standing not sure how to continue to feed the critters that surround me,

For my flesh have been eaten, you see.

My bones are being gnawed upon,

My will and my strength are almost gone.

I'm slowly turning to a walking tomb.

Let Me Have A Say

My body struggle to control the cage holding together the raging thoughts in my head.

They taunt me, yell at me, degrade me, betray me.

But still I stand, feigning happiness, hoping I can simply be:

Happy,

Carefree,

Me.

But alas I am only flesh, and the war in my head takes a toll on my body.

And even then, I say "don't worry"

I'll be…

And that's it.

I proceed to take forever and a day to say one phrase.

Sweating, stretching out and repeating syllabus,

Asking God to simply have a say.

And while I suffer and pray for a way,

My thoughts run deeper, wider…

Slowly eating me away.

II.

<u>Haiku - Progress</u>

bit by bit I creep

I long to extend my reach

perhaps then I'll teach

<u>Haiku - Step To Me Correct</u>

come to me correct

if you want to gain respect

as I am direct...

<u>Haiku – Women</u>

women are staples

merely an after thought ...

but, important enough

<u>Haiku – Teach Me</u>

teach me your ways child -

how to be truly carefree,

how to sleep in peace.

<u>Haiku – Black and Proud</u>

I am black and proud.

Black and a little too loud.

Pushing all buttons allowed.

<u>Dear whoever:</u>

I think I'm stuck in limbo. I know where I've been, I know where I want to go. But I'm not moving in the direction of anything. The progress is little. The trauma is overbearing. I need to move. Because; if I'm not moving, I might as well be dead.

III.

Did You See Her

Did you see her?
How she wore her crown?
Walking majestically, as if she was on sacred
ground.

Did you see her?
How she captured eyes from all around,
but yet never once did she make a sound?
Her crown adorned her face. a magical
Labyrinth of curls.
But gorgeous as it was, it looked out of
place.
Out of place because she would never win the
race.
She knew this, always did, yet she still walked
with grace.

Did you see her?
Her smooth ebony skin?
Glowing, yes glowing, from the moment she
walked in.

Did you see her?
Did you see her?!
Walked with no fear,
Proud of her hair,
Killed with her stare,
Did you see her?

<u>Unapologetic Woman</u>

Girl, can't you see?
Can't you see the goddess in you?
 It blinds me, its beauty is true.

Your skin, it glows and shimmer like liquid
gold.
Go ahead,
Wear something bold.

Pink, purple, blue,
You look beautiful in every hue.
Go ahead and grab that palate,
Go off and show your talent.

Yes, Wear that!
That bright eye shadow,
That lipstick,
Strut down that street like you own it.

Cause, you're far too beautiful to allow
someone to box you,
To tell you how to fix yourself.

You're a woman unapologetically
And you don't need anyone to tell you what you
need to be.

<u>Faded</u>

A shadow,
A mishap of who I use to be.
A figment,
So broken,
Is this really me?
Translucent,
Unnoticed,
What is my purpose?
The gloom, the doom
Is this now my home?
I'm slowly going bit by bit.
My existence,
Is this the end of it?
I try to call for help,
But no one cares.
I'm dead to them.
The girl who no one knew.
So I sit there willingly in my cursed doom,
For it is now what I call home.

<u>Hope</u>

A northern light,

A starlit night,

A silver flower,

A determined fighter.

As the plant grows in my soul,

It shouldn't be there, yet it holds.

A new surge of strength grows inside, I feel faint.

Before I know it, it begins,

casting all fears aside.

It can hurt me, disappoint me,

or even manipulate me.

But it grows,

It is determined to have its way.

So my body, in turn just obey.

Hope takes over, a deadly sin,

For when it starts it never ends.

Changed

Today she stands, one person,
divided in two.
The girl she sees, she does not know who.
For she is bitter calm and cold,
no more a little girl.

Her eyes are like bottomless pits
and words seldom leave her lips.
She has seen a lot, gain a lot,
but what she got, she wanted not.

The girl she was, the happy one,
the one who laughed and talked
while innocence shone in her eyes.
Was gone.

Locked inside so she can't be hurt.
She now watches and sees, always alert,
Never allowing herself to be hurt.
She knows what life can do to a person
and understands more than she shows.
She is smart, beautiful and cold.
Most of all she is changed.

Thank you for choosing to read Loud Thoughts

You can find me on the following platforms:

Facebook: @blackgirlpoet or @cachlinebooks (Author Cachline Etienne)

Instagram: @cachline_etienne

Twitter: @Cachline_E

Email: etiennecachline@gmail.com

Official Website:

authorcachlineetienne.wordpress.com

Other works:

Please note all works are available on amazon! Search Cachline Etienne on Amazon for all my works.

Teen Fiction

- Finding Mora
- Doubled Crossed
- Set Me Free
- Ammora
- Call Me Mora (Free Book)

Poetry

- Stories Untold
- Lipstick & Sneakers

Romance

- Visions of Her
- Learning Love (Coming 2022)

About the Author

Cachline Etienne is an Author, Poet and Artist born in the Bahamas. Her first book, a series of poems titled Stories Untold was published early 2018. To-date, Cachline is the author of eight published books. She writes in multiple genres, however her main/go-to genre is young adult fiction. Other notable genres are poetry and most recently, romance. Cachline's romance works are and will continue to be published under the pen name C. Etienne.

When asked, Cachline expresses that she writes to draw awareness and that her stories are not always tales of happiness. At any giving chance, Cachline advocates for love and equality. In her spare, Cachline prefers to read, write and paint. It is through reading; she discovered her love for Writing. Currently, Cachline Etienne is a Psychology major at the University of Bahamas. After university, Cachline plans to continue writing throughout her career.

www.ingramcontent.com/pod-product-compliance
Lightning Source LLC
Chambersburg PA
CBHW060920130726
48001CB00006B/2324